D0564921

Birthday presents

Story by Dawn McMillan

Illustrations by Naomi C. Lewis

On Friday, Matthew and Emma
went to the store
with Mom and Dad.

"Stay outside with Dad, Emma,"
said Matthew.
"Mom can help me
get your present first."

4

Matthew and Mom looked at the books and the toys.

Matthew saw the whistles. "Emma will like a whistle," he said.

"Oh, dear!" said Mom.

Matthew and Mom went outside.

"You stay out here, Matthew!"
said Emma.
"I'm going into the store now,
with Dad.
He can help me get your present."

Emma saw the whistles.

"I will get a whistle for Matthew," said Emma.

"Oh, dear!" said Dad.

After they got home,

Matthew hid Emma's present

in his room.

He shut the door!

Emma hid Matthew's present
in her room.
She shut the door, too!

On Saturday, Emma said,

"Happy birthday, Matthew!

Now we can open the presents."

"Happy birthday, Emma!"

said Matthew.

14

"A whistle!" said Matthew.

"A whistle for me, too!"
said Emma.

"Whistles are the best presents!"
said Emma and Matthew.